BALM FOR THE LIVING

poems by

Angie Minkin

Finishing Line Press
Georgetown, Kentucky

BALM FOR THE LIVING

Copyright © 2023 by Angie Minkin
ISBN 979-8-88838-218-9 First Edition
All rights reserved under International and Pan-American Copyright Conventions. No part of this book may be reproduced in any manner whatsoever without written permission from the publisher, except in the case of brief quotations embodied in critical articles and reviews.

ACKNOWLEDGMENTS

Thank you to the editors and publications that gave first homes to these poems (sometimes in earlier versions and forms):

"Star Drive in Yosemite"—*The MacGuffin*
"Sheltering Home"—*Vistas & Byways Literary Review* Honorable mention in 2020 Soul-Making Keats Literary Competition, Prose Poem Category
"Fifty Words"—*Rattle, Poets Respond*
"Pause"—*Birdland Journal*
"Evelyn, Unbending" Honorable mention in *Passagers* and published as "A Messenger"
"Paying Your Bills"—Honorable Mention in 2019 Soul-Making Keats Literary Competition, Prose Poem Category (Note: First two italicized lines are from The Gingko Light by Arthur Sze)
"Every Tear a Prayer"—*Unbroken Journal*. Awarded First Prize in 2020 Soul-Making Keats Literary Competition, Prose Poem Category
"Nettles of Dreams"—*Marin Poetry Anthology* (as "Transcendence")
"Jump Into Joy"—Erasure Poem from an Interview with choreographer Alonzo King, by George McCalman, 12/28/20 in the *San Francisco Chronicle*
"Unfinished Notes on Aging"—*Vistas & Byways Literary Review*
"Tango in Havana"—*Vistas & Byways Literary Review*
"Wonder"—*Pandemic Puzzle Poems Anthology*
"Old Lovers in an Older House"—*Dreams and Blessings: Six Visionary Poets*
"The Speaking of the Dream"—Note: Cento composed with lines from *Late Rapturous* by Frank X. Gaspar and *Sight Lines* by Arthur Sze
"Ode to Cedar Waxwings"—*Canary Literary Journal*

Publisher: Leah Huete de Maines
Editor: Christen Kincaid
Cover Art: *Calla Lily in a Glass*, by Janet A. Econome
Author Photo: Dan Sneider
Cover Design: Elizabeth Maines McCleavy

Order online: www.finishinglinepress.com
also available on amazon.com

Author inquiries and mail orders:
Finishing Line Press
PO Box 1626
Georgetown, Kentucky 40324
USA

Table of Contents

Feathers, Floating 1

Star Drive in Yosemite 2

Behind the mirror I hear my mother sing
"Too-ra-Loo-ra-Loo-ral" 3

Sheltering Home 4

Fifty Words 5

Considering Stars and Gases 6

Pause 7

Evelyn, Unbending 8

Paying Your Bills 9

Every Tear a Prayer 10

Nettles of Dreams 11

Jump Into Joy 12

When We Lived by the Sea 14

Repeated Observations of Starlight 15

Unfinished Notes on Aging 16

Tango in Havana 17

Wonder 18

Old Lovers in an Older House 19

The Speaking of the Dream 20

Ode to Cedar Waxwings 21

*For Dan, Jake, and Aly—with love and thanks
I couldn't have done it without you*

Feathers, Floating

Like my mother and grandmother, plucky
daughters of poor chicken farmers, I stand
at the sink, rinsing the cold, naked bird.
Grandmother extracted plumes one by one,
Mother singed tiny, errant pinfeathers—
generations of feathers, floating free.
My hands echo their deft motions, slicing
carrots and garlic, chopping celery.
I brown onions, skim off impurities.
In the dented soup pot, I conjure spells
to break high fevers, soothe despair, transform
the pale neck, liver, marrow, heart, and bones.
I can't resurrect the dead, but with each
golden drop, I seek balm for the living.

Star Drive in Yosemite

Just yesterday, I followed reverberations
of my meditation bell in trembling air
and remembered the purr of our white
mustang skimming the empty road
below Hetch Hetchy Dam. Top down, blasting
Beatles songs over the muscle car's growl.
Deep quiet when we stopped on that hot, dusty night—
Perseids showering us with gingko light, chimes
of our children hollering wishes to heaven.
Stars moving so quickly, our dancing children.
Was it the hokey pokey? And was it only the next day
we sculled up the Tuolumne in birch boats, rowing
as hard as we could? The children so much older now,
pulling ahead, glancing back—calling, calling.

**Behind the mirror, I hear my mother sing
"Too-ra-Loo-ra-Loo-ral"**

Behind the mirror, I hear my mother sing
"Too-ra-Loo-ra-Loo-ral"

while my father smokes, his smoke
fracturing the mirror light, the air now

silver and ragged beyond the mirror,
the window opens wide, but the blinds closed,

the room gray, his fingers fall soft
on the piano, he plays so softly, those hard

hands, Winston drooping in his mouth, shards
of notes, the same shards over and over,

note-shards that muffle the sparrow's cry
and whirl in my head, my hot head—

it is clear and still: no thwacks, no choking plums,
no belts. Inside the mirror my mother

is singing, I see her face shining, she carries a basin
of clear water. She kneels at my feet.

Sheltering Home

Rations, Liberty Loans and Victory Bonds. Armistice Day bells rang in war's end. Oh, joyous crowds, oh, raging infections. Quarantines, masks, schools closed. Too late for the rag pickers, paper carriers, chicken farmers on Denver's immigrant West Side. They kept working. My mother was three years old when her father died, flattened by flu's third wave, skin blue, blood on his pillowcase. My mother spoke little of the racking coughs, the wailing. My grandmother too poor to care for her children. The hands that pulled my mother away at the Sheltering Home for Jewish Children. My mother cried for her family, but often refused to speak during my grandmother's weekly Shabbat visits. Still, my mother learned to tap dance, wore white hair ribbons, ate boiled chicken and challah. It was quiet when my grandmother brought my mother home two years later, to the little house on Albion Street. The dog-eared photo of that day: my grandmother's slight smile, same as my mother's, the same soft eyes. My mother shuffle-ball-changed in little white anklets, called me dearie. On her deathbed, my mother looked up at her children, asked for her papa and the hard lemon candies he carried, her eyes already moving elsewhere.

Fifty Words
for Pancho

Imagine fifty words
to describe your world,
to define yourself,
your heart.
Imagine your thoughts
trapped like thousands of blue jays,
caught in a too-small cage,
wings battering iron bars.
Imagine no movement, decades of stillness.
You are inside this body, this corset
of bones and muscles, slack, useless.
You move your head and neck in residual
tics; hunt and peck so slowly,
it hurts you, but you persevere.
You type and you learn English, you learn French,
you graduate from high school.
All this after your accident at age 20,
all this after your devastating stroke.
All this after you can no longer move.
Imagine brilliant doctors who implant
a sensor in your brain and those 128 electrodes
pick up forgotten movements
of your vocal cords, your larynx, your throat.
Imagine a cable like a new umbilical cord,
linking your brain to the computer
that starts writing words. Your words.
The algorithm learns as you do,
and suddenly you have fifty words of speech,
racing from your brain waves to the screen.
What words do you need?
Hunger, thirst, hurt, good, bad.
Love, soul, heart.
Hug me. Kiss me.
Family.
Perseverance. Hope.
Tell me you love me.
Miracles.
Thank you.

Considering Stars and Gases
In honor of Yom HaShoah, Holocaust Remembrance Day

Forty light years away, six million shadows transit across stars, leaving clues, leaving behind dust and skulls. Here on earth, we observe, precisely measure masses of heavenly bodies, consider elements of iron, hydrogen, oxygen, carbon and consider the potency of other beings and the inner body, dare we say the soul?

Do six million souls leave a trail of stardust? A light beam of truth? To try and understand, I study faces in tattered photographs: Chana's smile is my mother's; Lev could be my father's twin; Esther's long fingers are mine. I hear babies crying, mothers shushing, see fathers shaking, knowing their arms cannot save their families—orders of magnitude that I cannot grasp, always the other, the horror, the questions. I carry them. It doesn't stop. I recite the Kaddish, lost in memory's turbulence—fragments, shreds, sequins. I imagine each body transmuting to energy, becoming infinity, or perhaps compressed to an infinitesimal point of singularity. Forty light years away, starlight wavers.

Pause

Tethered to the house, I polish
every mirror, hoping for new faces,
hungry for new air.

I climb to the blue water tower
behind your house. My three-year-old's
favorite walk. He used to skip ahead,

kicking pebbles, in tiny red-and-white
high-tops, just like his dad's.
Now he runs his own far-away trails.

A breath. The dusty scent
of blue gum eucalyptus pulls you
to unknown paths in woods so close to home.

On a cracked tree stump,
a pair of black high heels
splay in first position,

Whistles of an unseen thrush rise
on a collective sigh of cedars.
Four hawks spiral on afternoon currents.

Farther up the trail, a young father
cups his daughter's elbow
like an egg.

Evelyn, Unbending

I find myself hailing my neighbor as she trudges
past my house. Like the coast oaks lining our path,
Evelyn is unbending, her walker a prop to hold
dog treats, windbreaker, Cubs hat.
Small ghosts trail us.
Maggie, her devoted Jack Russell, long-gone.
Cricket, the coddled black-and-white mutt who died in April.
I try to stroke Evelyn's arm. She shakes
her head, eyes too bright behind thick lenses.
She tends our pets, waters our plants, knows everyone
within a mile of her little cottage. School kids
adore her front yard, decked out for holidays.
Gold and orange leaves, tiny Santas and elves,
red and blue paper flowers. Always pictures of small female dogs.
No one really knows Evelyn's story.
My pace slows to match hers as we walk up the hill to McLaren Park.
Evelyn's voice softens as trees blur and juncos flit overhead.
Did I ever tell you about the blue heron?
That bird stalked gophers with Cricket.
When Cricket died, damned if the heron didn't find me.
She looked me straight in the eye, then flew off.
Evelyn hands me a tissue, elbows tensed, almost barbed.
We retrace our steps in this origami life,
fold, open, rise in lines
of solitude that sometimes cross.
Look up, says Evelyn.

Paying Your Bills

*We long to shimmer in the darkness
with streamers*, you said, laughing,
when we met on the playground all those years ago,
trying to corral our little girls after school.

I flash on that moment,
now as I pay tall piles
of your unopened bills,

and I talk fast and slick
to convince PG&E to keep the lights on,
so your friends can toast you,
your daughter can hold your feet.

Then, I was thinking only of throwing
together mac & cheese for dinner,
helping with homework.

How could I move after I heard
you talk of brilliant streamers,
your hair flamed with gingko sun?

I stuttered *what, what, what,*
until you finally stopped
and stared straight in my eyes.
It's time to go home, you said.

Every Tear a Prayer

It never rains in LA, but today it pours. Your daughter knits warmth from fine Peruvian wool—night blues, slate gray, splash of orange. Her fingers can't stop. She tenderly tucks you in. Your son trims your beard, gently combs your hair, smooths your eyebrows. You always look so sharp. We toast you with Glenlivet 18, hot pastrami on rye, Kringles from the Danish bakery downtown. The bluegrass guitar and banjo send honey-prayers to all the gods. Bertie curls next to you, quietly guards your journey. She licks your hand as you take your last, sweet breath and slide between worlds. Breath of fire, breath of tears, breath of light. The full moon, the scudding clouds.

Nettles of Dreams

Old women stand at sinks, humming, shoulders
hitched back. Water thrums down, lonely floats up.
Sometimes the women sag under nettles of dreams.

Old women stare out kitchen windows, eat lemons,
tango with memories, eyes fog-narrowed, squaring
shoulders as they stand at sinks, humming

A kestrel lands in the hawthorn tree—
good luck or bad? Time, soundless, spirals
as the old women sag under nettled dreams,

and consider the dark—nearing. The dying sun,
rocks limned. Knives scrape potato parings,
and old women square up to the future, singing

of nothing, or perhaps lost children, folded
in black boxes, or perhaps tired ghosts,
these old women, humming private melodies.

Finches flash, winds hush. A quiet descends
on the kitchen. The women shuffle
as they wipe counters, tuck in long shadows,
these old women, humming, shoulders squared.

Jump Into Joy*

                                                        you are divine

artists

                                  keeping the mystery

everyone   is some kind of artist

                                        illuminating
                                        human beings
              luminescent souls   playing roles

                      moving   higher

on the

precipice   hell abounds   storm   brew

                churning   ∞   transformation

                    all that is dark and heavy   gotta go   →

          We are that   transition

                jump into joy now

the later game doesn't work

  single

minded   lead yourself into   victory

*Erasure Poem from an Interview with choreographer Alonzo King, by George McCalman, 12/28/20 in the *San Francisco Chronicle.*

When We Lived by the Sea

Surf spilled over a brown pelican's wing,
while we walked Ocean Beach. Laughed in light rain
and our kids raced waves, baked sand cakes, singing

to quick snowy plovers. We traced five rings
of sea glass, footprints—a labyrinth chain,
and surf swooped over the pelican's wing.

Fog faded. The sun broke through clouds that cling
to shore. A strong wind. We could breathe again
when the kids gathered close, sad, and singing

of kites lost in breakers with spools of string
tangled under water, twisted, and maimed,
while surf flew from the pelican's bent wing.

Grays and blues collapsed, prisms of nothing—
waves coated in black oil; wings soaked in pain.
Our kids dug hard to release the singing.

Those birds are gone, and silence is the thing
we grapple as we flail in this floodplain.
Once surf spilled from the pelicans' torn wings.
Our kids fledged. The sand echoes with singing.

Repeated Observations of Starlight
    for Leo

Forty light years away, seven rocky
worlds transit across a low-mass star,
leaving clues. Starlight dims, dips as exo-
planets orbit. Here on earth, we observe,
precisely measure masses of heaven-
ly bodies, consider elements, water,
consider carbon, oxygen, potential
for life. Potency of other beings.
We consider the inner body—
mystery of unknown masses. Few clues.
Body leaving body, leaving us bereft.
We fix our sights on the night sky, seeking
brightness. Forty light years away, do you
orbit? Does starlight dip when you arrive?

Unfinished Notes on Aging

Acid pools in the belly, bile in the liver, and these
bodies, some bodies, are these really our bodies,
curdle slowly as we age. Running creakily
down but not out. Denial not just a river and
every little part seems to crumble. Hey, we're
fighting to stay fit. Pretty good at playing the long
game of reinvention. It's so seductive and
holds such allure for our third eyes, our
inner children and all that woo-woo
jazz. Yes, we believe in chakras, energy fields,
kismet in a way. In healing light and
love for sure—at least for the masses.
Mothering the hungry might work and might
not be the worst idea. There are such
oceans of need on crazy Tenderloin streets.
Pity? Is that what we feel? Or perhaps a
quickening sense of there-but-for the grace, etc.
Redemption is what we pray for—if we pray
somehow, for someone. We've been protesting for all
time, it seems. The world worsens despite our actions.
Under water now, many of us. Underground too. We
visit our own internal demons, wondering
why we continue to struggle. We reach for
Xanax at night. Doesn't help. We meditate and practice
yoga at first light. Try hard to stay supple. Kick ass in
Zumba. And so we hope to keep on keepin' on.

Tango In Havana

We stumble up crumbling stairs

to meet Rodrigo, sinuous, slim,
a chiseled sneer. Claudia, twisted

black hair, slashes of red lipstick.
The maestros look

down at our matching tees, zip-
off khakis, thick-strapped sandals.

Rodrigo pulls me close, curls
me backwards. Claudia molds

your thighs just so with her knees.
We flounder, marooned penguins.

Our teachers shake heads, push
us together. I wince as you

step on my left instep, you curse
as I move forward instead of back.

We sigh as our torsos meld.
Thinner, younger.

Your knee thrusts my leg,
a precise diagonal.

I move to your breath.
Your stare lifts my chin

For eight long heartbeats,
flawless timing.

Wonder

I.
In Taiwan, an orange streamer,
massive, tentacles a three-year-old girl.
Her mother strains to anchor her daughter,
but the huge kite lifts high on powerful winds.

The kite yanks the child high in the air.
She rivers through clouds,
a dust mote on a python's tail.
Earth shadows zigzag like strobe lights.

Below, commotion,
as the child unfolds from the sky
and waterfalls to earth.
Safe again in her mother's arms.

II.
Does this little girl dream
of birds and clouds?
Do her shoulder muscles twitch,
as her arms flutter like wings?

Does she ache to surf wind echoes,
eyes dark with yearning?
Will she only wear orange?
Does she always look skyward?

III.
In San Francisco, I wake
to my orange cat's unblinking stare.
Trapped behind my front window,
I fold swans from paper squares.

I long to dream with this child.
Among smoke scrolls and haze,
I search the sky for runes of her flight.

Old Lovers in an Older House

We've been lovers for forty years.
We still dance slow.
Life moves so fast.
We strolled with gleeful babies,
who giggled when we raced.
We ran with kids on bikes,
as they chanted the mantra you taught them:
I know how to ride a bike; I know how to ride a bike.
We white-knuckled the San Francisco hills
with new drivers and bought many new clutches.

So much life lived in the walls
of this little saltbox house.
100 years old and showing its age—
earthquake cracks,
shreds of ancient paisley wallpaper.
We burned white sage
in my mother's abalone shell,
smudged corners and shadows
to purify the space and dispel drugged ghosts.
We splashed sun on the walls upstairs
and warm green in the kitchen
to bring the trees inside.
Our kids have never known another home.

We're aging fast now—
those steep steps stare us down.
Is that the shadow of a pale horse?
You beat the drums.
I'll burn more sage.

The Speaking of the Dream
Cento for Frank X. Gaspar and Arthur Sze

So many years later, on a coast, waves rolling to shore,
light everywhere and the old stars gleaming over the burying fields,
in the sky, not a shred of cloud.
You can almost hear the heavens opening.
Choirs of angels out in the eucalyptus trees but beyond it all you hear nothing,
By then the light had lengthened in deep angles,
our shadow hearts beating through us, the yellow flurry of the moths.
This is the writing, the speaking of the dream.
I could see the burdens of love grinding in the bodies.
Moon waxes—the bones drop, my brush is sharp.
I step out of the ditch but step deeper into myself.
Tracks of moonlight run ahead of where I can be,
now I block the past by writing the present.
The arc of our lives is a brightening then dimming. Once I thought
I wanted my heart to grow until the world would sit
inside it like a bright egg.

Ode to Cedar Waxwings

Black-crested and yellow-dipped, you arrive
to show us how to feast fully. The being of you,
the life of you, too many to count,
you gray-silked, juice-addled gluttons.

You chatter and gorge on the toyon berries,
red and dripping from the tree that emerged
by magic—a city-sized beanstalk, a miracle
from a seed dropped, perhaps, by your ghost-mother.

Thick, bronze leaves shadow my backyard Buddha
as the fruit falls in his lap. He smiles at the neighbors
as they hack the branches hanging over the fence.
How they hate the stains stuck on their cement yard.

Don't they know this native endures?

I hush, freeze—try to spy. You startle,
rise as one, your wings beating.
You settle on phone wires, until the cat sleeps,
the sun drifts, and you can't resist the lure

of those siren seeds. You'll carry the leathery pods,
release them in another garden in another time,
and another woman will wonder
where did that tree come from?

Branches stripped, you ascend, tiny scraps
of fog, quiet now in the wind's hustle.
I climb on top of my Buddha's shoulders,
check my back for sprouting feathers.

With Thanks

So many thanks are due to my family and friends for their love and endless support, to my teachers and mentors for their inspiration and generous encouragement, and to my writing groups for never tiring of the work. I have found a wonderful community in poetry!

Ellen Bass, Katie Ford, Diane Frank, Kathleen McClung, Michael Morse, Erin Redfern, and Brian Tierney are unbelievable poets, gifted teachers, and warmhearted mentors.

I am so grateful to my various writing crews: Abby Caplin, Annis Cassells, Emily Darby, Suzanne Dudley, Mary Ellison, Heather Saunders Estes, Elsa Fernandez, Cecile Garcia, Lisha Adela Garcia, Laura Garfinkel, Marian Enochs Gay, Kathryn Santana Goldman, Cie Gumucio, Judith Hansen, Jennifer Read Hawthorne, Kathe Jordan, Elise Kazanjian, Anna Kodama, Nancy Lee Melmon, Robin Michel, Irene Nelson, Sharon Pretti, Christine Penney Riovolan, Christy Shephard, Leonora Simonovis, Sharon Smith, Lynn Tait, Holly Veldhuis, Ann Orr Weil, and Ellen Woods. All of you talented poets rock! And how can I thank Janet Econome for her gorgeous artwork and Nancy Econome for her technical wizardry? Thanks also to Gary Schoofs and Dan Sneider for their beautiful photos.

Angie Minkin is a San Francisco-based poet who stands on her head for inspiration. Angie has volunteered as a poetry editor of *Vistas & Byways Literary Review*. Her work has been published in that journal, as well as *The MacGuffin, Rattle, The Poeming Pigeon, The Unbroken Journal, Persimmon Tree, Rise Up Review*, and several others. Angie is a coauthor of *Dreams and Blessings: Six Visionary Poets*, published in 2020 by Blue Light Press. Her poems have been included in *Fog and Light, San Francisco through the Eyes of the Poets Who Live Here* and *Pandemic Puzzle Poems*, also published by Blue Light Press. She has won awards in the Soul-Making Keats Literary Competition in the Prose Poem and Sonnet Categories, and in the Journeys Category of the Ina Coolbrith Circle Annual Contest. Angie is inspired by the political landscape and the voice of the wise woman. Some of her favorite authors include Elizabeth Alexander, Ellen Bass, and Jane Hirschfield. In addition to writing, Angie practices yoga, takes dance classes, and travels to Oaxaca, Mexico as often as possible. www.angieminkin.com

www.ingramcontent.com/pod-product-compliance
Lightning Source LLC
Chambersburg PA
CBHW022128090426
42743CB00008B/1058